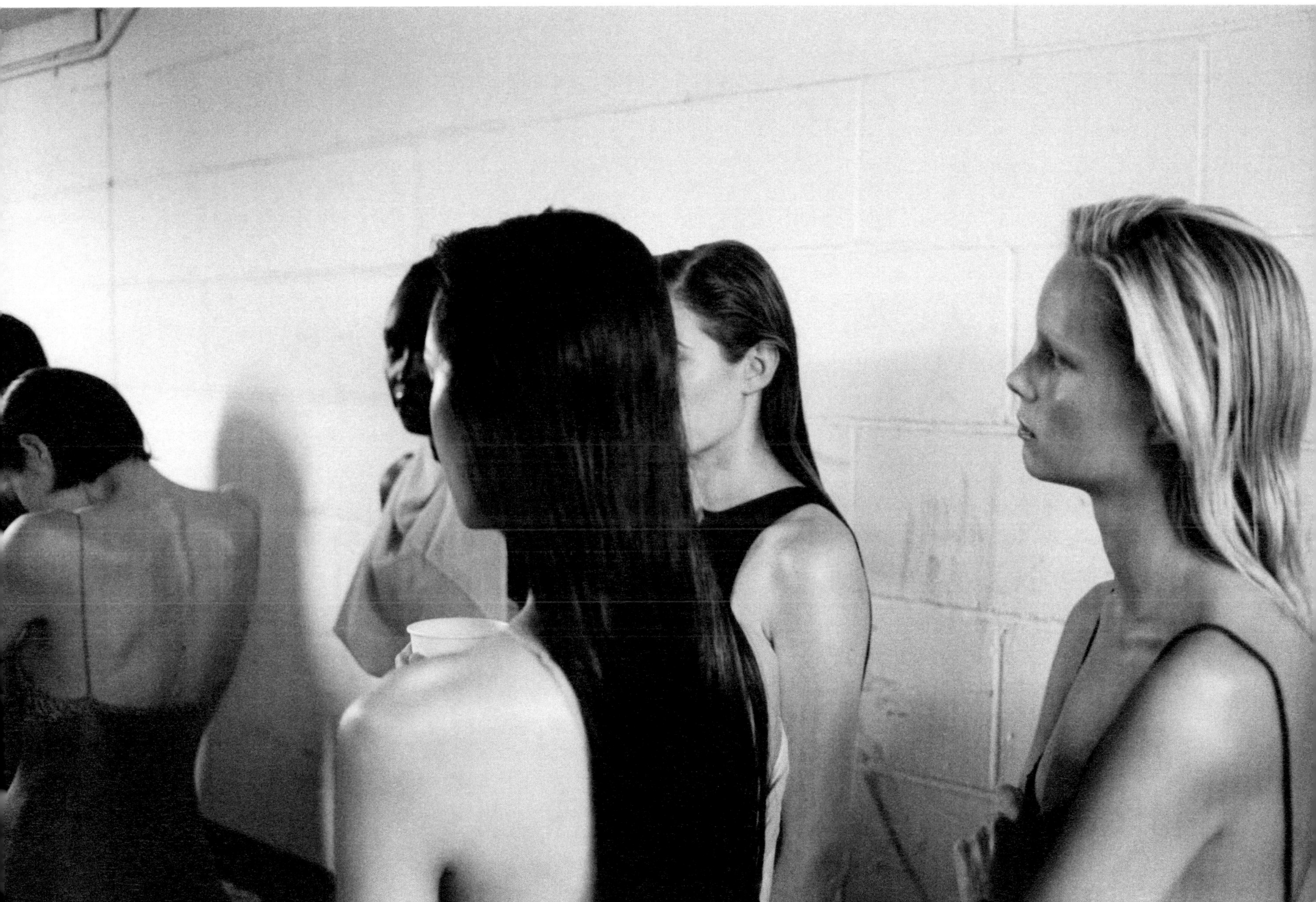

SUPRIYA LELE
ANDERS EDSTRÖM
London, Barbican Centre
18 September 2023

Printed in 2023
Edition of 250
Photography by Anders Edström
Styling by Jane How
Creative Direction by Jonny Lu
Art Direction and Design by Emily Schofield at Jonny Lu Studio

ISBN 978-1-8380354-4-0

SUPRIYA LELE STUDIO CREATIVE DIRECTOR Supriya Lele, CEO Donald Ryan, CREATIVE CONSULTANT AND SHOW DIRECTION Parinaz Mogadassi, BRAND MANAGER Caitlin Price, K
DESIGNER Jaimee Mckenna, PATTERN CUTTER Evan Phillips, ATELIER COORDINATOR Bella Wynne, PRODUCTION MANAGER Victoria Craven, FITTER Louise Holsgrove, BTS PHOTOGRAPHERS
Kennedy Doig, Billal Taright, RUNNERS Charles Wisnec, Josef Back, VOLUNTEER DRESSERS Abbie Giles, Eleni Hulme, Nuha Dhorajiwala, Ellie Butler, INTERNS Daisy Day, Kate Ignatyeva, Shanique Bailey, C
Johnson, Stella Nieto Berghusen Foppianon Day, Indi Jones, Daisy Williams, Lyra Cherry, Sachika Bhojani, Sophie Dee. JONNY LU STUDIO ART DIRECTOR Jonny Lu. AI PR FLOATING Adam Iezzi, FLOATI
BLOCK A UK PRESS Antonio Pignone, DOOR Martha Weaver, Lianne Hatterseley, Molly Doherty, BLOCK A REVIEWERS Jakob Ashton, BLOCK A VIP Kyle Knowles, GUIDING GUESTS AT BARBICAN Fra
Reffell, Michael Hassan. STYLING STYLIST Jane How (AGENT Brigitte Sondag at Art Partner, PRODUCER Eeva Evula at Art Partner), ASSISTANTS Katie Shaw, Elle Britt, Nathan Fox, HEAD DRESSER So
Bell at Blæd Agency, DRESSERS Inca Bayley at Blæd Agency, Patience Boateng at Blæd Agency, Nina Garhen at Blæd Agency. HAIR HAIR STYLIST Cyndia Harvey (AGENT Chloe Deforges at Art Partner, PRODU
Anna Fielding at Art Partner), ASSISTANTS Harry Reynolds, Apranji Kerketta, Sasha Kluvitse, Verity Smiley Jones, Emilie Bromley, Becca O'Neil, Rita Skomorova, Karolina Saunders, Rosie Grace Smith, Rac
Banjo, Erika Neumann, Leanne Millar, Anastasiia Gryniuka, Karen Bradshaw, Adeswa Awobadejo, Tsuyoshi Tamai. MAKEUP MAKEUP ARTIST Fara Homidi (AGENT Ayesha Arefin at The Good Company F
PRODUCER Hanna Gear at The Good Company Reps), ASSISTANTS Jason Case, Cristine Dupuys, Francesca Leach, Laisum Fung, Megumi Matsuno, Naomi Nakamura, Samanta Falcone, Simona Svantner
Sogol Razi. MANICURE MANICURIST Adam Slee (AGENT Sasha Respinger at Streeters), ASSISTANTS Abena Robinson, Veronica Butenko, Rebecca Orme, Georgia Hart, Amy Thomas, Amy Atkins. CAST
CASTING DIRECTOR Jess Hallett (AGENT Brigitta Toyoda at Streeters, PRODUCER Em Midwood at Streeters), ASSISTANT Julia Gilmour, MODELS Adele Ruboneka, Akuol Deng, Cheyenne Tichich, Cyr
Wu, Esme Cornelius, Iveth Ventura and Kate McNamara (AGENTS Rosie Ware and Jovita Zavisiute at Milk Management), Africa Garcia, Edna Karibwami, Kerolyn Soares, Laura Reyes and Mary Ukech (AGENT
Asher at IMG), Barathy Akkan (AGENT Joe Katt at Kult London), Bente Oort, Suzune Oda and Tara Halliwell (AGENT Gemma Green at Models 1), Celina Ralph, Fanfan, Huiji Chen, Migoa Guol and Sara Caba
(AGENT Jahale Jureidini at Elite Model), Cora Corré (AGENT Kristina Louise Philpot at Tess Management), Devyn Garcia (AGENCY DNA), Eliza Rutson Pang and Evie Harris (AGENT Chris Yianoullou at Pre
Model Management), Sophia Enggaard (AGENT Ash Mosley at Present Model Management). SHOW CALLERS SHOW CALLER Matt Barksby at Sourced, BACKSTAGE MANAGER Bethan James, BACKST
ASSISTANT Paola Glec. PHOTO & VIDEO RUNWAY PHOTOGRAPHER Chris Yates, BACKSTAGE PHOTOGRAPHER Anders Edström (AGENT Imogen Crosby at Artistry, PRODUCER Jess Rodgers at Artis
VIDEOGRAPHER Ethan Lodge. SOUND MUSIC SUPERVISION Samuel Strang. PRODUCTION/FARAGO PROJECTS EXECUTIVE PRODUCER Sylvia Farago, PRODUCERS Nicola Caterall, Elsa Puangsu
PRODUCTION MANAGER Tommaso Albertini. PRODUCTION COORDINATOR Seline Matei, ASSISTANTS Tommy Aucott, Brandon Young, Gloria Cialfi, Eryn Baxter, Alec Jafrato, Mark George, Mark Shiel